How Do Planets Move?

What Will Happen?

Sonja Reyes

COMPUTER SCIENCE For the REAL World™

Rosen Classroom™

Published in 2018 by The Rosen Publishing Group, Inc.
29 East 21st Street, New York, NY 10010

Book Design: Jennifer Ryder-Talbot
Editor: Caitie McAneney

Photo Credits: Cover Vadim Sadovski/Shutterstock.com; p. 4 xtock/Shutterstock.com; p. 6 (laptop) Andrey_Popov/Shutterstock.com; p. 6 (planets) cigdem/Shutterstock.com; p. 8 3Dsculptor/Shutterstock.com; p. 10 BestPhotoPlus/Shutterstock.com; p. 12, 14 Santhosh Varghese/Shutterstock.com.

ISBN: 9781538352342
6-pack ISBN: 9781508136873

Manufactured in the United States of America

CPSIA Compliance Information: Batch #WS18RC: For Further Information contact Rosen Publishing, New York, New York at 1-800-237-9932

Table of Contents

Around and Around

Can you feel the Earth moving? You most likely cannot. However, Earth is turning each day and orbiting, or moving around, the sun. Each of the planets in our **solar system** turns and orbits the sun. Planets are far away from us and we can't see most of them. How can we learn about their movements?

What's in a Solar System?

Our solar system includes the sun and all the planets around it. The major planets are Mercury, Venus, Earth, Mars, Jupiter, Saturn, Uranus, and Neptune. There are also smaller space bodies, such as asteroids and moons. You can look at a map of our solar system to see what it looks like.

Solar System Models

People have learned a lot about planets through telescopes and **spacecraft**. We know what each planet looks like. Science museums often have models, or small copies, of the planets. The models can show you what the planets are like. A model of the solar system can show you where each planet is located.

What Happens in Space?

People have tracked the motion of the planets for hundreds of years. However, now we can look at **simulations** to see what those motions really look like. You can find simulations of how the planets move on your tablet or computer. You can also see a simulation at a **planetarium**.

Neptune

Making a Solar System

You can make your own solar system simulation. Draw pictures or build a model of each of the planets and the sun. You are the sun. Give a planet to eight of your friends. Then, have your friends line up in order of their planet's distance to the sun. Make the planets orbit the sun in a circle.

Learning From Simulations

What do planet models and simulations tell you? Each orbit of the sun is a year for that planet. If you look at a simulation of planets moving, you can see which ones have the longest and shortest years. You can also see the distance between planets and the sun. Simulations bring space down to Earth!

Glossary

planetarium: A building or room where people can watch images of space.

simulation: An object or event that shows or acts like another object or event.

solar system: The sun and all the space objects that orbit it, including the planets and their moons.

spacecraft: A vehicle that travels in space.

Index